FOREWORD ∞

This booklet charts the remarkable transformation of Clayton in the nineteenth century from a rural landscape on the fringe of Manchester to a heavily industrialised area, which specialised in manufacturing chemicals for the textile industry. The mass production of new chemicals and processes made the Clayton chemical industry of national importance. Other industries vied for space there, including textile mills, collieries, and brick manufacturers, linked by a canal network; and there was still room for numerous workers and their families to live in houses of various sizes.

By the end of the second millennium, however, the area was blighted by derelict factories and toxic waste. Over the last few years, a scheme of land

CON...

reclamation and regeneration has once again transformed the landscape so that it is now difficult to imagine the heavy industry that once existed there. It is therefore important to record the industrial remains and history for the benefit of future generations. In challenging environmental conditions, archaeologists have successfully undertaken a series of targeted excavations, which help to tell the story of Clayton's historical development. The results of these archaeological investigations, the history of the area, and the industrial processes that once took place, are ably presented in this booklet.

'Coal, Cotton, and Chemicals' is the ninth volume in the *Greater Manchester's Past Revealed* series. It complements the work undertaken by Oxford Archaeology North on another former industrial landscape during remediation of land beside Manchester City's stadium: 'Rediscovering Bradford: Archaeology in the Engine Room of Manchester' (*Greater Manchester's Past Revealed* **4**).

NORMAN REDHEAD, Heritage Management Director,
Greater Manchester Archaeological Advisory Service

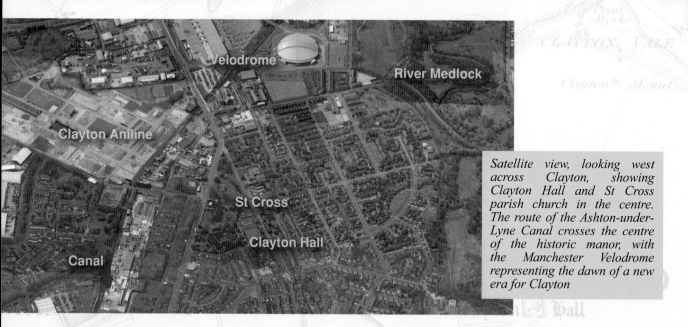

Satellite view, looking west across Clayton, showing Clayton Hall and St Cross parish church in the centre. The route of the Ashton-under-Lyne Canal crosses the centre of the historic manor, with the Manchester Velodrome representing the dawn of a new era for Clayton

Clayton lies in East Manchester, situated some 3km to the east of Manchester city centre, with Bradford to the west and Openshaw to the south. Formerly a manor in the historic township of Droylsden, Clayton was absorbed into Manchester in 1890 and, in 1896, formed part of a new North Manchester township. The natural topography has a fairly level terrain, which falls to the north through Clayton Vale and the River Medlock. Clayton Brook flows along the southern boundary of the manor, separating Clayton from Openshaw.

Settlement in Clayton can be traced to at least the twelfth century, when the timber-framed Clayton Hall was erected as the manorial seat of the Clayton family. This impressive manor house and associated estate was occupied through the centuries by several famous Manchester families, including the Byrons and the Chethams. Whilst parts of the hall were altered or rebuilt in the seventeenth and eighteenth centuries, the surviving buildings and the surrounding moat nevertheless provide an evocative reminder of Clayton's medieval origin. The lofty parish church of St Cross, situated immediately to the east of the hall, also makes a strong contribution to the historic character of the area. Designed by William Butterfield, one of the leading architects of the Gothic Revival in English architecture, the church was built in 1862 and served a population that was increasing rapidly as a result of the industrial growth of Clayton.

Aside from agriculture, the earliest large-scale industry in Clayton was coal mining. Coal had been extracted from thin seams near the surface for generations, but by the end of the eighteenth century shafts were being sunk to exploit the deeper seams and production increased dramatically. The most important of the local coal mines was Clayton Colliery, which was sunk in *c* 1790, and was served by a private branch of the Ashton-under-Lyne Canal. The main line of this canal opened in 1796-7 to provide an important transport link between Ashton-under-Lyne, Oldham and Manchester. The canal took a route across the heart of Clayton, and stimulated the growth of new factories and works along its corridor.

Various industries were established in Clayton during the second half of the nineteenth century, although the area became noted as a key centre for producing chemicals that were needed by textile manufacturers, particularly those engaged in the dyeing and printing trades. The most famous of these chemical works was undoubtedly Clayton Aniline, where analine and a range of synthetic dyestuffs were produced for national and international markets. This works was founded in 1876 by Dr Charles Dreyfus, one of the leading chemists of his age and a notable figure in the history of synthetic dyes. It was the third aniline works to open in Manchester, and became one of the largest and most significant chemical works in England.

Aerial view of Clayton Aniline in 1951. Whilst it had already become one of the largest single factory sites in the Manchester area, the works continued to expand during the 1950-60s, and benefited from a multi-million pound investment that equipped the site with new buildings and state-of-the-art plant

OMG Works

Clayton Aniline

Belsize Works

Aerial view across the site of Clayton Aniline and the adjacent OMG chemical works in 2011, during an initial stage in the remediation works (©www.SuaveAirPhotos.co.uk)

Amongst the notable industries that came to Clayton towards the end of the nineteenth century were the Manchester Cycle Manufacturing Company, and Belsize Motors Ltd, which produced the first motor car to be built in Manchester. By 1950, however, this factory had been subsumed by further expansion of Clayton Aniline, which eventually sprawled across 12 hectares in the south-western corner of the historic manor.

The demise of Manchester's manufacturing industries in the second half of the twentieth century left large tracts of disused land across East Manchester, and contributed to the economic decline of the area. The final closure of Clayton Aniline in 2007, and the adjacent OMG chemical works in 2010, added considerably to the amount of derelict industrial land in the area. However, the major regeneration projects that were carried out for the Commonwealth Games in 2002, which led to the creation of the world-class sporting facilities enjoyed in the area today, have provided a flagship for the wider renewal scheme for East Manchester. Building on the significant economic benefits brought to the area by this renewal, Manchester City Football Club, working in partnership with Manchester City Council, developed a scheme for the regeneration of Clayton Aniline and adjacent derelict land. As an essential initial stage, remediation works were required to treat soils that had been contaminated by the site's intensive use for manufacturing chemicals, and to remove associated buried structures.

These essential remediation works would inevitably destroy any buried remains of the former factories and associated workers' housing, remains that could potentially yield important evidence for their historical development. Consequently, the Greater Manchester Archaeological Advisory Service (GMAAS), which provides advice to Manchester City Council, recommended that an archaeological investigation of the site was undertaken prior to the ground works. This was carried out by Oxford Archaeology North (OA North) in 2010-12.

A series of trial trenches was excavated across the site in the first instance. These were targeted on Clayton Colliery, its branch canal and associated buildings, together with the sites of a cotton mill, a fire-brick works, and various forms of workers' housing. The footprints of Clayton Aniline and the adjacent Clayton Chemical Works were also targeted by the trial trenches, and whilst important remains were discovered, considerable challenges were faced by working in an environment that had been heavily contaminated by these former industries.

The trenches also showed that the buildings around the former pit bank at Clayton Colliery had been destroyed entirely, together with the structural elements of the infilled branch canal, but the remains of the cotton mill, the fire-brick works, the chemical works and several blocks of workers' housing were of sufficient interest to merit further excavation. This was intended to make a full record of any remains prior to their ultimate loss. The exciting findings from these archaeological excavations are presented in this booklet, which also summarises the industrial development of the historic manor of Clayton.

Location of trial trenches and excavation areas placed across the sites of Clayton Aniline and the OMG chemical works

0   200 m
1:5000

·5·

Virtually nothing is known of the early history of Clayton, although some settlement in the area had become established by the twelfth century. Clayton formed the western part of the historic township of Droylsden, which comprised 1621 acres (656 hectares) to the south of the River Medlock. Clayton was the only manor in the township, and was separated from Droylsden proper by Edge Lane, which linked Openshaw with Newton via a crossing of the River Medlock at Clayton Bridge. This is thought to have been an ancient fording point, whilst a bridge is known to have been in use by 1696.

Clayton contained the inferior hamlets of West End and East End, and there were also cottages at Clayton Bridge, although the early settlement was almost certainly focused on Clayton Park in the centre of the manor. At the heart of this estate was Clayton Hall, which was occupied in the twelfth century by the Clayton family. The size of the population of the manor at this time is unknown, although it was undoubtedly very small.

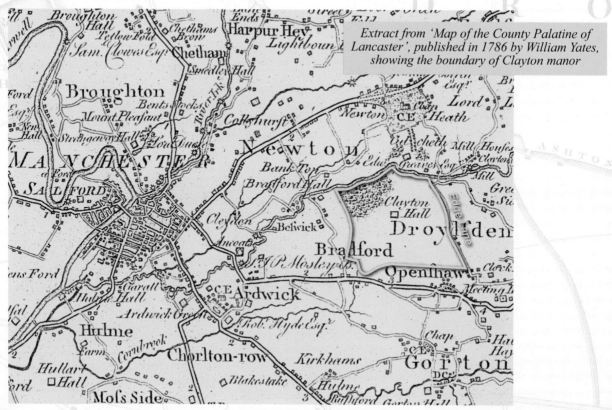

Extract from 'Map of the County Palatine of Lancaster', published in 1786 by William Yates, showing the boundary of Clayton manor

Clayton Hall

Clayton Hall was built in the twelfth century, and comprised a quadrangle of two acres that was encompassed by a broad and deep moat. This was crossed originally by a wooden drawbridge, although it was replaced at an early date by an elegant two-arch stone bridge. The hall passed from the Claytons to Richard Byron in 1194, and remained in his family until 1620, when Sir John Byron decided to sell his Lancashire estates to settle numerous debts.

The Clayton estate was purchased by George Chetham, a grocer of London, and his younger brother, Humphrey, a successful local merchant and chapman. Occupied initially by George Chetham, the hall became the principal residence for Humphrey following the death of his brother in 1627. Humphrey Chetham is widely acknowledged as one of Manchester's best-known philanthropists and famously bequeathed its hospital and library, which is now the world-renowned Chetham's Music College. He also became an advocate of the Parliamentary cause during the English Civil Wars (1642-51) and, according to local tradition, Oliver Cromwell spent three nights at Clayton Hall during the conflict.

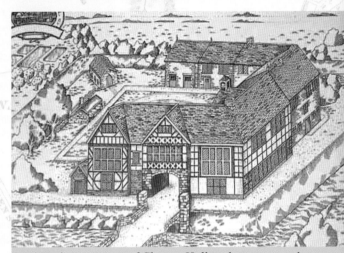

Artist's impression of Clayton Hall in the seventeenth century, showing the main L-shaped range, outbuildings, and a small chapel in the north-west corner, which had been licensed for services in 1400 (illustration by Mike Pendry Design, email: mike.pendry@googlemail.com

Humphrey Chetham died in 1653, and the Clayton estate passed to his eldest nephew and heir, George Chetham. The hall was still by far the largest residence in Droylsden township at that time; 93 hearths in the township were liable for taxation in 1666, of which 18 were in Clayton Hall. Situated a short distance to the south-east of the hall was the Fold, an enclosure of approximately four acres. This contained three timber buildings, designated as the wheat barn, the oat barn, and the great barn. The oat barn was reported to be a fine example of a cruck-framed building, being 116ft long and 25ft wide (35.35 x 7.62m) and containing six pairs of timber crucks. This barn was demolished in *c* 1877, whilst the great barn had burnt down in 1852.

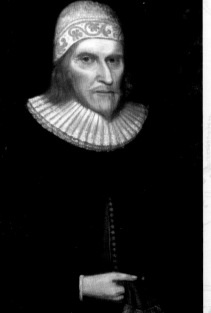

The only known portrait of Humphrey Chetham (1580-1653)

Clayton Hall remained in the hands of the Chethams until 1769, when it passed via marriage to the Greene family. Part of the hall was demolished in the eighteenth century, and was replaced by a simple brick wing. It became the residence for a succession of local worthies and, during the later nineteenth century, a series of rectors of St Cross parish church. In 1897, the hall was acquired by Manchester Corporation, which carried out extensive restoration works, with an intention that it might be converted for use as a Humphrey Chetham Museum. Whilst this never materialised, it is presently a living history museum that is used as an educational resource for local schools.

The rear of Clayton Hall in 1896, with the moat in the foreground. The hall still survives, and is afforded statutory protection as a Grade II* listed building and a Scheduled Monument. The oldest surviving structure on the site is the sandstone bridge across the moat, whilst parts of the building probably date to the fifteenth century, with sixteenth- and seventeenth-century alterations (Manchester Archives and Local Studies)

Early Industrial Development

Clayton retained its medieval character into the eighteenth century, with a small population that was engaged primarily in farming, although historical sources also refer to some coal mining and the cottage-based production of textiles. The land was divided into small farm holdings, and the main crops were grass or hay, together with wheat, oats, potatoes and turnips. This agricultural landscape persisted into the nineteenth century, although most of the population had abandoned their farming lifestyle by the middle of the century; it was reported in 1793 that 100 acres of wheat were sown in Clayton, but this had been reduced to none by the 1850s. This transformation of the local economy was a direct result of the rapid industrialisation that was centred on Manchester, coupled with Clayton's position on the southern edge of the Manchester Coalfield and the benefits of transportation afforded by the Ashton-under-Lyne Canal and the completion of the Ashton New Road turnpike in 1825.

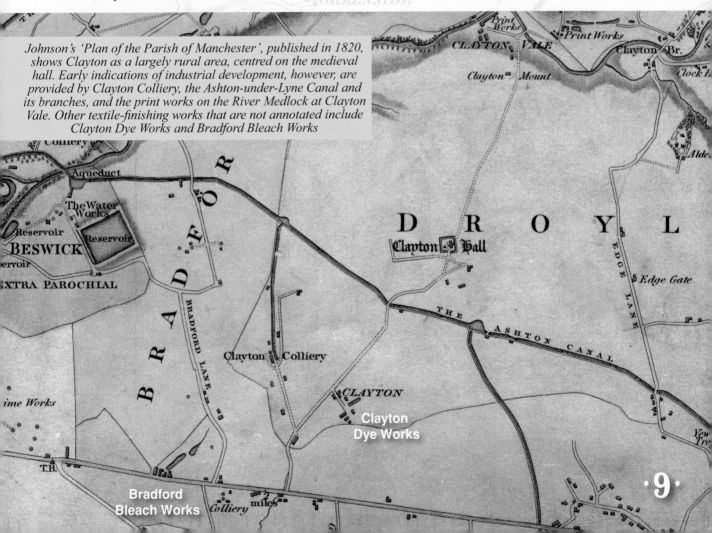

Johnson's 'Plan of the Parish of Manchester', published in 1820, shows Clayton as a largely rural area, centred on the medieval hall. Early indications of industrial development, however, are provided by Clayton Colliery, the Ashton-under-Lyne Canal and its branches, and the print works on the River Medlock at Clayton Vale. Other textile-finishing works that are not annotated include Clayton Dye Works and Bradford Bleach Works

Aside from agriculture, one of the first industries to develop in Clayton was coal mining. The earliest coal pits were certainly in use by the seventeenth century, and will have probably exploited the thin seams of coal that lay close to the surface. The exponential growth in demand for coal from the eighteenth century, coupled with improvements in pumping technology, led to the sinking of shafts to exploit the deeper seams. The largest of these deep mines in the manor was Clayton Colliery, which was established in *c* 1790. Very little is known of the origins of the colliery, although it was owned from an early date by John Thornely of Clayton Hall, who traded as John Thornely & Co. The growth of the colliery was undoubtedly stimulated by the completion of the Ashton-under-Lyne Canal, to which the pit bank was connected via a private branch canal. The canal will have provided an essential transport route, and may also have been used as a drain for the colliery, receiving water pumped out of the underground workings.

Following the death of John Thornely of Clayton Hall in 1818, the colliery was operated for several years by John Thornely of Dodworth near Silkstone, but it was taken over in the 1820s by a partnership between Charles Barrett, John Bradbury and Silas Leigh, trading as the Clayton Colliery Ltd. Bradbury and Leigh went on to purchase land at Biddulph in Staffordshire in 1831 to establish the Bradley Green Colliery, and also owned collieries at Haughton and Hyde in Cheshire.

Writing in 1828, John Bradbury noted that the workings at Clayton were much deeper than those of the adjacent Bradford Colliery, raising concerns of flooding from their neighbour. According to Bradbury, Clayton Colliery had three shafts in 1828 and most of the coal was extracted via No 3 Pit from the Two Feet Mine, although plans from the 1840s show that the overlying seams were also mined extensively.

Bradbury also noted a preference to transport the output of the colliery from just one of the shafts in order to save the expense of constructing additional wharves. The pit bank developed around No 1 Pit, or the Engine Pit, where the coals were sorted before being loading into canal boats.

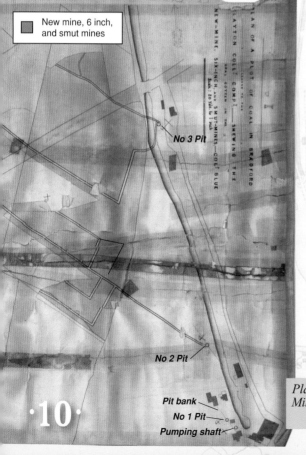

New mine, 6 inch, and smut mines

No 3 Pit

No 2 Pit

Pit bank
No 1 Pit
Pumping shaft

Plan of 1841, showing the underground workings in the New Smut Mine, with details of structures on the surface taken from an estate plan of 1836 (reproduced courtesy of the Coal Authority)

In 1829, a tremendous explosion that resulted in several fatalities in one of the pits was reported. Miners traditionally illuminated the underground workings using candles with open flames, which was the principal cause of triggering the explosion of flammable gases. Considerable efforts were expended in the early nineteenth century to devise a solution, culminating in the introduction of the miners' safety lamp, which enclosed the flame and prevented it from igniting any flammable gases. There is some dispute over who invented the first safety lamp, although William Clanny is accredited with establishing the principle of separating the flame from the surrounding atmosphere in 1813. Whilst Clanny failed to apply this breakthrough to a practical lamp, this was achieved successfully in 1815 by both Sir Humphrey Davy and George Stephenson. However, neither of these new safety lamps eradicated the threat of explosions entirely, and numerous deaths from firedamp explosions at Clayton Colliery were documented by the Mines' Inspectors during the 1850s and 1860s.

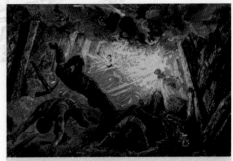

An engraving published by Louis Simonin in 1868 showing a firedamp explosion underground

Clayton was one of the few collieries that did not employ women at the coalface prior to the Mines and Collieries Act of 1842, which prohibited all females and boys under ten years old from working underground. At that time, the colliery employed 80 adult men, 26 men between the ages of 13 and 18, and ten boys under the age of 13. It was also in the early 1840s that Charles Barrett retired from Clayton Colliery Ltd, leaving John Bradbury and Silas Leigh as the sole owners.

Bradbury and Leigh continued to extract coal from the Four Feet Mine, the Yard Mine, the New Mine and Smut Coal seams to the west of the pit bank during the 1840s. They also paid some attention to the rich deposits to the south.

Plans held by the Coal Authority chart the progress of the workings to the south of the pit bank during the second half of the nineteenth century. These show a network of underground haulage roads and shafts between workings that extended at different levels beneath the neighbouring townships of Bradford and Openshaw.

A section through the coal seams at Clayton Colliery, produced in 1878 (reproduced courtesy of the Coal Authority)

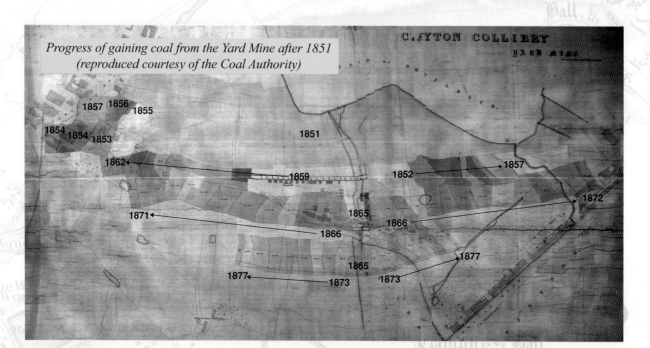

Progress of gaining coal from the Yard Mine after 1851 (reproduced courtesy of the Coal Authority)

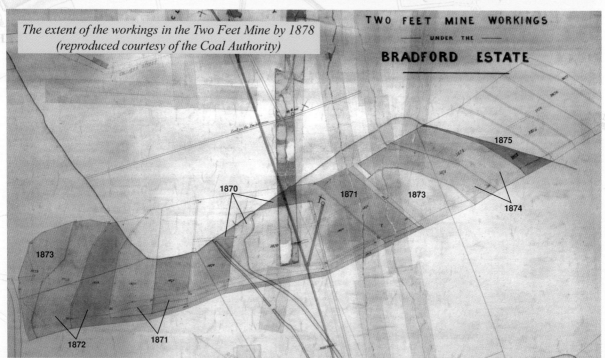

The extent of the workings in the Two Feet Mine by 1878 (reproduced courtesy of the Coal Authority)

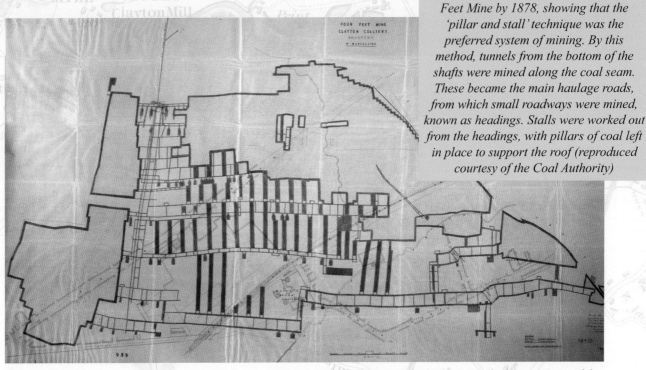

The extent of the workings in the Four Feet Mine by 1878, showing that the 'pillar and stall' technique was the preferred system of mining. By this method, tunnels from the bottom of the shafts were mined along the coal seam. These became the main haulage roads, from which small roadways were mined, known as headings. Stalls were worked out from the headings, with pillars of coal left in place to support the roof (reproduced courtesy of the Coal Authority)

By the 1850s, the company's collieries at Clayton, Haughton and Hyde were being managed by the son of John Bradbury, also called John, whilst the Bradley Green Colliery in Staffordshire was managed by his brother. John Bradbury retired in the 1860s, and Clayton Colliery passed to his nephew, another John Bradbury, who had been born in Staffordshire but took up residence on Coal Pit Lane in Clayton.

It was during this period that lamp checks began to be used at collieries. Each miner was issued with a check token, which was usually taken home at the end of a shift. The token was handed to the lamp man at the start of a shift and exchanged for a safety lamp stamped with the same number as on the check. In the event of an incident, this system enabled rescue services to ascertain how many miners were underground.

The business partnership between Bradbury and Leigh was dissolved in 1877. Clayton Colliery was managed for a short while by John Ridings, who lived next door to John Bradbury on Coal Pit Lane, but it closed in 1878. The surface buildings were demolished shortly afterwards, and the Ordnance Survey map of 1893 provides no trace of this once-important colliery.

An early example of a brass lamp check, bearing the name 'Clayton Colliery'

The Ashton-under-Lyne Canal was promoted by a group of local businessmen, including several colliery owners, who intended to build a canal between Ashton-under-Lyne and Manchester, with branches to Stockport and Hollinwood. It was also to connect with the Peak Forest Canal at Dukinfield, providing the limestone quarries near Dove Holes and the huge lime kilns at Marple with a vital transport link to Manchester.

Work commenced in 1792, although it was several years before the canal company appointed Benjamin Outram as their consulting engineer 'in order to better bring about its completion'. The main line from Ashton-under-Lyne to Manchester was opened in 1796, with the branch to Stockport being completed in the following year. Several private branch canals were also built, of which those to Bradford and Clayton Colliery were the most prominent. The Bradford branch was not completed to its full length until the early 1840s, but the Clayton branch was opened before 1820. This was crucial to Clayton Colliery, and also stimulated the development of other industries along its short length.

The Clayton and Bradford branches of the canal, shown on the Ordnance Survey map of 1848 (surveyed 1845)

The Clayton branch remained in use following the closure of the colliery in *c* 1878, and does not appear to have been abandoned completely until the 1960s. The canal was finally infilled during the 1970s, and much of its route sealed beneath concrete to provide hard surfacing for the OMG chemical works.

A rare view along the Clayton branch canal from its junction with the main line in 1960, showing Ashton New Road bridge and the chimney of the Clayton Chemical Works (Manchester Archives and Local Studies)

The Canal-Side Building

The sequence of nineteenth-century maps of the area depicts a small rectangular building amongst the growing number of industrial premises adjacent to the canal. The purpose of this building is not known from the documentary records available, although the form in which it is shown on some maps suggest that it was a row of three workers' cottages.

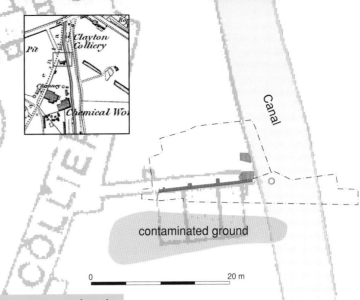

Excavated area superimposed on the Ordnance Survey map of 1893

The remains of the northern wall of the canal-side building

The footprint of the building, together with the route of the infilled canal, was targeted by the initial trial trenches. This showed that the canal had been destroyed entirely, and whilst most of the building had been removed by later development, the foundations for its northern wall survived. These remains were fragmentary, but it was nevertheless clear from the width of the wall and the apparent addition of buttresses that the building had been of a fairly substantial construction, and inconsistent with the design of workers' housing.

Two detached brick-built structures were also discovered during excavation. These were situated on the former bank of the canal, and may have been foundations for cranes that were used for loading and unloading boats. With these considerations in mind, it seems possible that this had been a canal wharf, with the building perhaps providing warehouse accommodation, or stabling facilities for the colliery or Clayton Chemical Works.

The origin of the textile industries in Clayton is poorly documented, although weaving linen was probably supplementing the income from agriculture for many inhabitants as early as the sixteenth century, and the bleaching of textile goods was being carried out in the area during the reign of James I (1603-25). By the end of the eighteenth century, when the cotton industry throughout Lancashire began to expand at an unprecedented rate, there were numerous hand-loom weavers in Clayton and Droylsden, producing fustian, checks and linen goods.

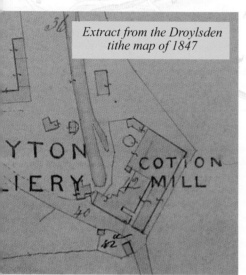

Extract from the Droylsden tithe map of 1847

The first textile factory in Clayton was the Clayton Vale Print Works, which was established on the River Medlock in 1798. Other textile-finishing works in the area included Clayton Dye Works and Bradford Bleach Works, which are both shown, but not annotated, on Johnson's map of 1820. However, very few steam-powered cotton mills were built in Clayton. The earliest documentary reference to a cotton mill in the manor occurs in a newspaper article of 1837 that reports the bankruptcy of John Gore, a flax spinner at Clayton Mill. The precise location of Gore's factory is uncertain, although it may have been the building marked 'fustian mill' on the 1848 Ordnance Survey map, and shown as a cotton mill on the tithe map of 1847. However, writing in 1859, Higson considered this mill to have been established in the late 1830s by Messrs J Leigh & Sons, which is likely to have been the same family that had interests in Clayton Colliery.

The tithe map shows that the mill occupied a site between the end of the branch canal and a road heading south to Clayton Lane. The complex is depicted as several adjoining ranges, which probably included a weaving shed, warehousing and office accommodation, and the power plant. A small detached building and a circular structure in the northern part of the site may have been the gas plant. Of particular interest is the narrow channel that leads off the canal, immediately to the north of the building, presumably representing a conduit for supplying the mill with a source of water.

The remains of Clayton Mill exposed beneath the mound during initial trenching

The remains of the brick chamber for a waterwheel

The site of the mill was targeted for investigation as part of the archaeological works carried out in 2010-12. Much of the building's footprint was buried beneath a huge mound of material dumped during the later twentieth century. Approximately 6500m^3 of material was removed from this mound to enable some initial trenches to be excavated across the south-western part of the mill, which revealed well-preserved elements of the steam-power plant.

Further excavation unearthed a series of foundations that yielded important evidence for the development of the mill's power system. The earliest fabric included a brick-built structure that almost certainly represented the remains of a waterwheel chamber. This chamber was capable of housing a substantial waterwheel, with a maximum diameter of 26ft and a width of 5ft (7.92 x 1.52m). It seems probable that the water to power the wheel had been supplied via the narrow channel leading from the canal, but all physical remains of this headrace had been removed completely. Whilst the surviving canal warehouse at Portland Basin on the Ashton-under-Lyne Canal contains a hoist that is powered by a waterwheel, using water drawn from the canal, Clayton Mill is a rare, if not unique, example of such an arrangement being applied to a cotton mill.

Water exited the wheel chamber via a 5ft (1.52m) wide brick channel, which seemed to terminate in a small reservoir that lay beneath the floor of the mill. This reservoir had been largely destroyed by later development, and it remains unknown how the water was managed from this point. It is tempting to suggest that it was pumped back to the canal, as it is difficult to understand how the water level in the canal would otherwise have been maintained, although firm evidence for any such system is lacking.

The restored waterwheel at Portland Basin

Clayton Mill was taken over in 1856 by the firm of Benjamin Clarke & Co, listed as 'cotton manufacturers' in trade directories for the period. In 1878, the mill was leased to John Bradbury of Clayton Colliery, but was taken over in the early 1880s by William Shawcross, who operated 320 power looms. Excavation revealed that the waterwheel had been abandoned by this time, and its chamber infilled and remodelled to enable a steam engine to be fitted. The remains of foundation beds for this steam engine were exposed adjacent to the waterwheel chamber, and were of a layout consistent with that required by a beam engine.

The excavated remains of the foundation beds for a steam engine installed in Clayton Mill

Excavation in the south-western corner of the mill, immediately adjacent to the engine room, revealed the remains of the boiler house, where the steam required by the engine had been raised. The layout of the excavated remains indicated that the boiler house had contained two Cornish boilers. The foundations for a hexagonal-shaped chimney were discovered immediately to the rear of the boilers, but this could not be excavated fully due to contaminated ground conditions.

William Shawcross was registered as a debtor in 1896, and the mill passed to the Clayton Mill Company for a few years, but had fallen into disuse by 1908. The buildings were demolished shortly afterwards, and the site used as a dump for waste from the adjacent chemical works.

The excavated remains of the boiler house

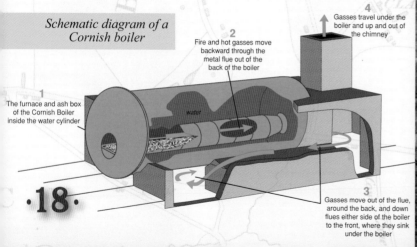

Schematic diagram of a Cornish boiler

1 The furnace and ash box of the Cornish Boiler inside the water cylinder

2 Fire and hot gasses move backward through the metal flue out of the back of the boiler

3 Gasses move out of the flue, around the back, and down flues either side of the boiler to the front, where they sink under the boiler

4 Gasses travel under the boiler and up and out of the chimney

water

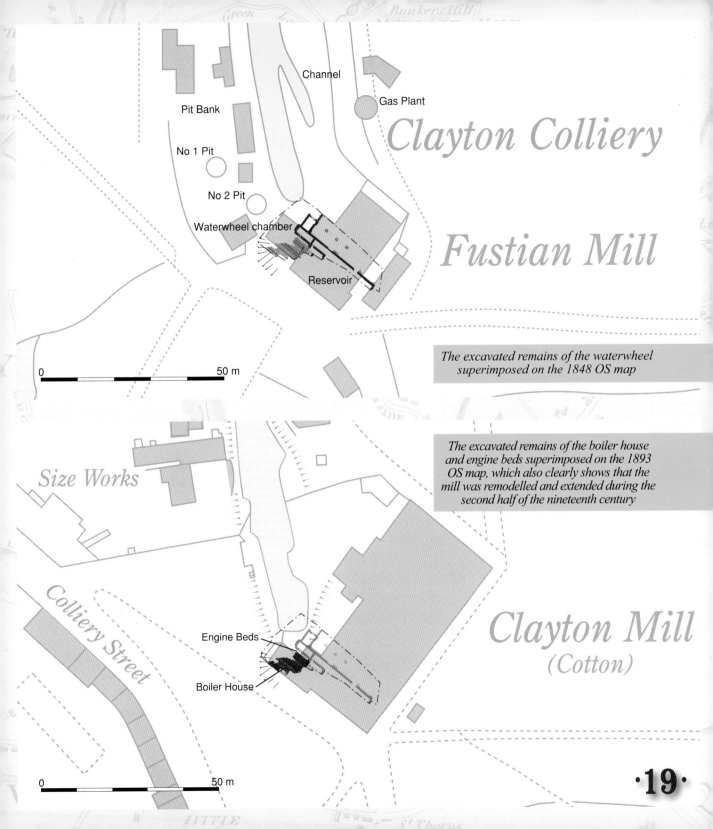

Channel

Gas Plant

Pit Bank

Clayton Colliery

No 1 Pit

No 2 Pit

Fustian Mill

Waterwheel chamber

Reservoir

0   50 m

The excavated remains of the waterwheel superimposed on the 1848 OS map

The excavated remains of the boiler house and engine beds superimposed on the 1893 OS map, which also clearly shows that the mill was remodelled and extended during the second half of the nineteenth century

Size Works

Colliery Street

Engine Beds

Clayton Mill
(Cotton)

Boiler House

0   50 m

The application of chemistry played a crucial role in Britain's phenomenal industrial growth during the nineteenth century. Commercial chemistry had been practised on an industrial scale in England since the late sixteenth century, when alum began to be manufactured from natural shale, and copperas was being produced from the atmospheric oxidation and hydrolysis of iron pyrites. Alum was crucial as a mordant, which 'fixed' dyes to textile fabrics, whilst copperas was intended primarily for the production of ink or black dyes. A large expansion in the manufacture of copperas in the eighteenth century was stimulated by a growth in demand for the materials that could be made from it. In particular, the heating of copperas produced an oily liquid known as 'oil of vitriol', or concentrated sulphuric acid.

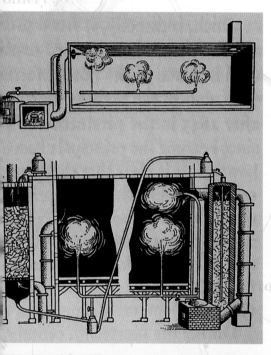

The lead chamber process of producing sulphuric acid in the late eighteenth century. A charge of sulphur and nitre was introduced upon two trays, which was lit and allowed to combust and then condense. This process was repeated over a period of weeks, after which the acid was withdrawn and concentrated in lead vessels

The availability of sulphuric acid became of key importance to the development of several different industries during the late eighteenth and nineteenth centuries. A more efficient means of producing sulphuric acid had been achieved by John Roebuck, who pioneered the use of leaden condensing chambers and, in 1749, established the first sulphuric acid works based on the process at Prestonpans in Scotland.

Soda ash was another important chemical product for which demand increased significantly during the nineteenth century. It was an essential ingredient for many manufacturing industries, and especially the production of soap and glass. Several patents had been obtained in the late eighteenth century by British chemists intent on manufacturing alkali to provide a synthetic alternative to natural sources of soda and potash. However, it was a process patented by Nicolas Leblanc in 1791 that was adopted widely, and particularly in England after 1824, when the repeal of the salt tariff enabled this crucial natural ingredient to be bought cheaply.

The Leblanc process involved heating salt and sulphuric acid to form sodium sulphate, often referred to as 'salt cake'. This was heated with coal and calcium carbonate, usually chalk or crushed limestone, to produce 'black ash'. Soda ash was then extracted by leaching the black ash with warm water, and concentrating the resultant solution through evaporation.

By 1852, when annual production had reached 140,000 tons, Britain was by far the largest producer of soda ash in the world. Inevitably, this was at some cost to the environment. By-products included hydrochloric acid gas, which was vented into the atmosphere, and an insoluble solid waste known as galligu. This had no economic value, and was piled in heaps or spread on vacant land near the soda works, where it weathered to release hydrogen sulphide, a toxic gas giving an odour of rotten eggs.

The Leblanc process of producing soda ash was superseded by the Solvay process, which was introduced in the 1860s, although a few Leblanc works remained in operation into the twentieth century. Amongst these was the works situated on the east bank of the branch canal, just to the north of Clayton Mill, which was established by CJ Schofield & Co in 1864. Soda production ceased there in 1914, leaving a gigantic heap of galligu, known locally as the 'mucky mountain', as a legacy of 50 years of production. The 'mucky mountain' was finally removed in 1951-3 to enable an expansion of the Clayton Aniline works.

Another important branch of the chemical industry that developed gradually in the nineteenth century was that based on the fractional distillation of coal tar and extraction of its various chemical components. In this process, the coal tar was heated, and the different chemical compounds with their various boiling points were collected individually as they evaporated. Gas works generated large volumes of coal tar as a by-product that was considered in the early nineteenth century to have no economic value. However, technological innovation in the second half of the century enabled coal tar to become the principal raw material for synthetic dyestuffs, which provided an alternative to natural sources of dyes and revolutionised the textile-finishing process.

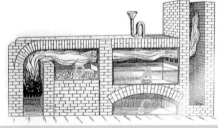

A section through a salt-decomposing furnace. Salt and sulphuric acid were brought together in a lead-lined chamber (A). Hydrochloric acid was driven off by chemical reaction, which was completed in the hottest part of the furnace (D), and the resultant black ash was collected in C.

Black ash vats, in which the sodium carbonate was dissolved out to produce soda ash

Soda works

Waste mound

Aerial photograph taken in 1951 looking south across the site of CJ Schofield's soda works and the mounds of process waste

Clayton Aniline and the Birth of Synthetic Dyes

Charles Dreyfus (1848-1935)

The first synthetic dye was discovered by accident in 1856 by WH Perkins, who found that a rich purple dye could be produced by reacting aniline with potassium dichromate, and then extracting the dye by adding alcohol. The immediate success of aniline purple, or mauveine as it became known, paved the way for the introduction of a range of synthetic dyes. These included aniline black, the formation of which was discovered by John Lightfoot of Accrington in 1863. This process was of especial value to calico printers, who rapidly became prolific consumers of aniline. It was against this background of a burgeoning demand for aniline that the Clayton Aniline Company was founded in 1876 by Dr Charles Dreyfus, a 28-year-old chemist from the Alsace region of France.

The Company immediately leased 5400 square yards of land in Clayton, situated between the newly laid-out Chatham Street and the Ashton-under-Lyne Canal, and built a small factory for producing aniline oil and aniline salts for local calico printers. The works went into production in 1877, and comprised a range of buildings along the canal, and another range fronting onto Chatham Street, with aniline being manufactured in a shed occupying the centre of the site.

The canal-side buildings included a naptha shed, where solvents were produced from the fractional distillation of coal tar. These solvents included benzol, which was converted into nitrobenzol through the addition of nitric acid. Other buildings in this range included the mirbane shed, which housed the nitrobenzol, together with a nitric cake shed and the saltpetre shed. The buildings along Chatham Street included stables, offices, the boiler house, a smithy, and a shed for the production of aniline salts. The works' chimney was situated at the western end of this range, with the nitric acid shed along the western boundary of the site.

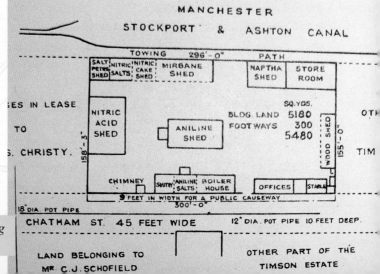

Extract from a lease of 1877, showing the layout of the original works

This historic core of the works was targeted for archaeological investigation in 2011, and trenches were placed across the footprint of the aniline production shed, the boiler house, the aniline salts shed, the smithy and chimney. The trench placed across the aniline production shed revealed part of a brick floor, but the excavation was curtailed by hazardous volatile gases that were released from the ground. It was, however, possible to excavate the remains of the aniline salts shed, the boiler house and the works' chimney.

Excavated remains of the aniline salts shed, with the foundations for the chimney to the rear

Stacked bricks in the flue beneath the aniline salts shed

The foundations of the boiler house had been damaged during twentieth-century development of the site, although a section of the arched, brick-built flue to the chimney survived intact. The southern part of the floor for the aniline salts shed, which lay originally between the boiler house and the chimney, had been carefully sited over this flue, with additional smaller flues branching off beneath the northern part of the floor. This had presumably been intended to provide the building with under-floor heating and ensure that the aniline salts remained dry. The flue had been remodelled on several occasions, which seemingly included the stacking of bricks in a chequer work pattern inside the flue. These bricks will have absorbed the heat from the exhaust gases generated by the boilers, and will have helped to provide a source of constant warmth for the overlying building.

Excavation also revealed the well-preserved remains of the original chimney, which comprised a brick-built, square base measuring 3.45m across. The octagonal-shaped throat of the chimney was 1.75m wide, and had been lined with a single skin of fire bricks. In addition to the flue that lay beneath the aniline salts shed, the fabric of the chimney retained physical evidence for two other flues, although these had become redundant and were bricked-up in the twentieth century.

The foundations for the original works' chimney

1: Nitric Acid Shed
2: Smithy
3: Aniline Salts Shed
4: Boiler House
5: Aniline Production Shed
6: Mirbane Shed
7: Saltpetre Shed
8: Naptha Shed

9: Store Room
10: Wood Shed
11: Office Block
12: Stables
— Area investigated by excavation

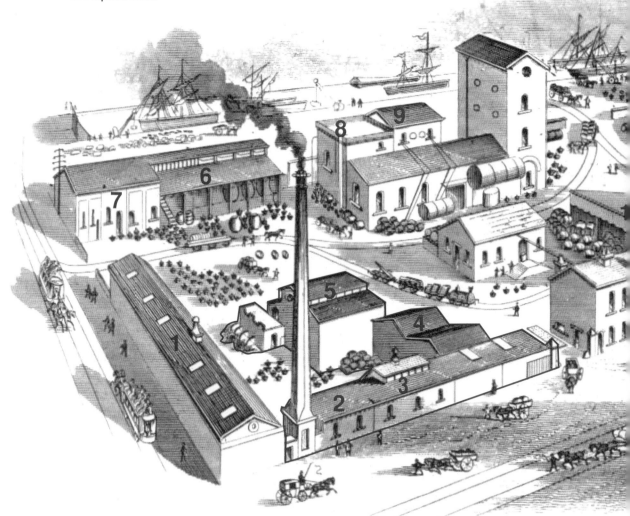

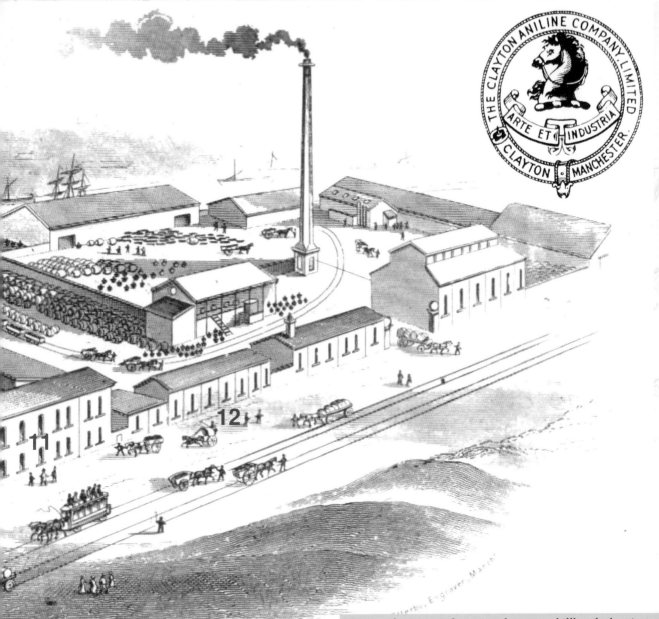

THE CLAYTON ANILINE COMPANY, LIMITED.

ARTE ET INDUSTRIA

CLAYTON · MANCHESTER

Extract from an early twentieth-century billhead, showing the historic core of the Clayton Aniline works. Whilst this provides an accurate depiction of the buildings, some artistic embellishment has been applied to peripheral features, such as the vessels on the canal.

Significant progress in the development of synthetic dyes was achieved during the 1880s, following the work of Paul Bottiger in Germany. Bottiger discovered in 1884 that cotton could be dyed directly with a synthetic dye that he had produced without first treating the fabric with a mordant, thereby streamlining the process considerably. Another direct dye, known as primuline, was introduced in 1887 by Arthur Green, who at that time was working in London. Green's dye was of a different chemical structure from that of Bottiger, and could be treated on the fibre and combined with a range of components to provide several colour shades.

Arthur Green

Pattern card of early direct dyes produced at Clayton Aniline

The Clayton Aniline Co., Ltd.

CLAYTON YELLOW G.		
CLAYTON GELB G.		
JAUNE CLAYTON G.		

CLAYTON YELLOW.
CLAYTON GELB.
JAUNE CLAYTON.

NITROPHENINE.
NITROPHENIN.
NITROPHÉNINE.

PIECE.   STÜCK.   PIÈCE.

Realising the potential of these new products, Dreyfus began to develop his own range of direct dyestuffs. Despite achieving some success, however, the dyestuffs department at Clayton remained very small initially, and the principal products continued to be aniline oils and salts. However, in 1894, Dreyfus offered Arthur Green the position of managing his fledgling dyestuffs department at Clayton. Green accepted, and during the next seven years he made significant progress in extending the range of dyes produced at Clayton. This required substantial capital investment, and in order to raise the necessary finance for new buildings, the Company went into voluntary liquidation in 1897, and a new company with the same name was floated with an increased share capital.

CLAYTON ANILINE COY LTD
CLAYTON, NEAR MANCHESTER.
Aniline Manufacturers.

Insurance Plan of Clayton Aniline of 1898, showing the buildings on the north side of Chatham Street

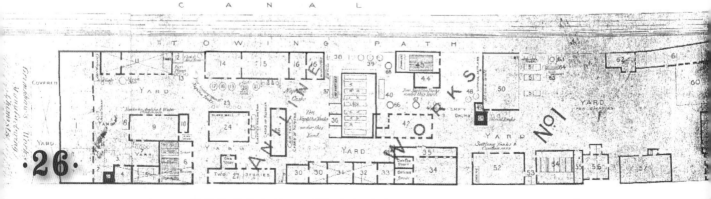

British dye makers were facing increasing competition from Continental manufacturers by the end of the Victorian era, and whilst the Clayton works maintained a favourable position in the aniline market, the dyestuffs department contracted following the departure of Arthur Green in 1901, and was partially closed in 1907. In the same year, the Patents and Designs Act was passed. This legislation compelled foreign dye firms which had been granted British patents to obtain production facilities in Britain. The Clayton Aniline Company soon entered

A view across Clayton Aniline in c 1920, showing the newly laid railway along Chatham Street

into discussion with European firms that had expressed an interest in acquiring the Clayton factory as a manufacturing base and, after several years of negotiations, the Society of Chemical Industry in Basle (SCI Basle) purchased a majority of the Company shares and took control in 1911.

Charles Dreyfus resigned from the Company in 1913, whilst the outbreak of war in 1914 caused further upheavals at Clayton Aniline, not least as six senior members of staff were interned as foreign nationals. The war also generated a huge demand for high explosives, and Clayton Aniline was requisitioned by the Government to increase output of trinitrotoluene (TNT). An Act of Parliament backed by the Ministry of Munitions was passed during this period to enable a railway to be built to the works, which proved to be of immense benefit in later years.

In 1918, the Basle Community of Interests was formed, which comprised the chemical-manufacturing giants of the Sandoz Chemical Company, JR Geigy, and SCI Basle (later CIBA), the owners of Clayton Aniline. This combination, through technical and commercial collaboration, enabled the production of dyestuffs at Clayton to be reinvigorated, and the factory was expanded during the inter-war years. Whilst the Second World War caused a shift in the Company's focus, a plan virtually to rebuild Clayton Aniline was drawn up in 1957. This had been implemented by the mid-1960s, creating a 57-acre site that employed more than 2000 people. Aniline production, after which this famous company took its name, ceased in 1965 and synthetic dyes became the dominant product.

The Clayton Aniline Company was experiencing severe financial problems by 1980, forcing the temporary closure of its works. The final closure was announced in 2004, and this huge site had been decommissioned by 2007.

The main process floor in the azo dyes manufacturing plant that went into operation in 1963

·27·

Clayton Chemical Works

One of the earliest chemical factories in the area was the Clayton Chemical Works, which occupied a site on the western side of the branch canal. This works was established in 1837 by Charles Joshua Ronchetti, a 'manufacturing chemist', who appears to have been concerned primarily with the distillation of coal tar to produce naphtha. This was obtained by heating coal tar in a still, and condensing the vapours that were released at different temperatures. The resultant products were then subject to refinement to produce the chemicals required.

The fractional distillation of coal tar was pioneered in Britain, initially in 1815 by FC Accum, and latterly by GD Longstaff in 1822, who were seeking to obtain naphtha. The principal use of naphtha at that time was in the manufacture of rubber goods, which was pioneered on a factory basis by Charles Macintosh, who established the world's first commercial rubber factory on Cambridge Street in Manchester in 1824-5.

The Ronchetti family continued to operate the Clayton Chemical Works into the 1850s, although it had been taken over by John Bethel & Co before 1860. John Bethel had been a pioneer of coal-tar distillation, and in 1838 patented a process for preserving timbers using 'heavy oil' fractions. The demand for timbers preserved in this manner rose greatly with the expansion of the railway network. Bethel & Co also manufactured a range of other products at their Clayton works, including cake alum, Epsom salts and naphtha, although the firm was declared bankrupt in March 1886.

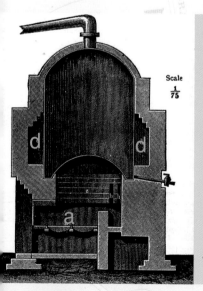

Scale $\frac{1}{75}$

Cross-section of an early coal-tar still. Hot gases generated from burning coal on the fire grate (a) were led via the flue (d) around the wrought-iron still, which contained the liquid coal tar. Pipes fitted to the top of the still provided an outlet for vapours and an overflow during filling. Stills were often fitted with pipes for the injection of steam, which acted to stir the tar and also helped to carry off the vapours formed during distillation. The vapours were condensed in coolers or a condensing worm. Waste pitch gathered at the bottom of the still, and was drawn off via a tap or valve

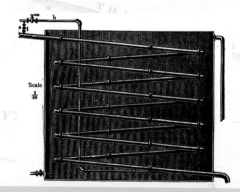

Scale $\frac{1}{40}$

Cross-section of a condensing worm. A first fraction, or 'light oil', was taken at temperatures of up to 210°C. The second fraction was the 'middle oil', obtained by boiling up to 240°C, and contained most of the carbolic acid and naphthalene. The next fraction was the 'heavy oil', or creosote, and the final fraction was obtained at a temperature of around 270°C. Above that temperature, 'anthracene oil' was obtained up to the completion of distillation.

The works was taken over subsequently by Hardman & Holden Ltd, which was established primarily to manufacture sulphuric acid, but also carried out tar distillation. In 1934, the company expanded through the acquisition of other businesses, including CJ Schofield and Manchester Oxide Co, and began to produce paint-drying chemicals and Manchester gum, which was used by adhesive-label manufacturers. The firm was taken over by Borax Holdings in 1960, which in turn merged with RTZ in 1968. Following restructuring subsequently, the business was acquired by OMG Inc in 2001.

The site of the Clayton Chemical Works was targeted for archaeological investigation in 2012. Whilst parts of this site were heavily contaminated, and thus could not be excavated, buried remains in the centre of the former works were available for investigation. This enabled the foundations for the works' chimney to be exposed and recorded, together with the boiler house, processing areas and several large below-ground storage tanks.

The Ordnance Survey map of 1848 marks a chimney in the approximate position of the excavated foundations. However, some of the component bricks were stamped 'BC', indicating that they derived from the Bradford Colliery brickworks and had thus not been produced prior to the 1870s. This chimney measured 5.7m across, and was of an octagonal form that was characteristic of later nineteenth-century construction.

High-level view across the excavated remains of the Clayton Chemical Works

Exposed foundation of the chimney

Excavation of the northern part of the area revealed the well-preserved remains of a boiler house, which contained the settings for two Lancashire boilers. These had been 30ft (9.14m) long, consistent with the largest type of boiler available in the late nineteenth century. When in operation, the boilers would have been charged with fuel at their northern end, as the remains of the flue to the chimney survived at the southern end, together with housings for butterfly control-valves that will have regulated the draught passing through the boiler. The fabric of the flue incorporated several bricks bearing the Bradford Colliery 'BC' stamp.

Excavating the remains of the boiler house (GMAAS)

The setting walls comprised a combination of refractory and machine-made bricks, with a lining of refractory bricks. The flame beds were entirely of refractory bricks, some of which for the western boiler were stamped 'HAMMOND', indicating a post-1890 construction date. The bricks used in the eastern boiler setting, however, included 'NETTLE' fire bricks, which probably post-dated 1930, suggesting that this boiler had been replaced during the inter-war years.

A section excavated across the eastern boiler bay showed that the flame bed was two-brick courses thick, and had been placed on a concrete surface. The exterior elevations of the boiler setting-walls had been insulated with a 0.5m-thick deposit of sand, which had been partially vitrified through prolonged exposure to high temperatures.

Section excavated across one of the boiler settings

Fire brick produced by William Hammond at Pott Shrigley in the Poynton Coalfield of East Cheshire. These bricks were produced from the 1890s until 1968.

Other Chemical Works

The archaeological works carried out at Clayton Aniline and the Clayton Chemical Works have provided a snapshot of a key industry that came to dominate the local economy by the late nineteenth century. The density of these chemical works is depicted clearly on the Ordnance Survey map of 1893, which shows a concentration along the corridor of the Ashton-under-Lyne Canal. These included the Canal Chemical Works, operated by the Grimshaw Brothers, which lay on the south bank of the canal and adjacent to Clayton Aniline. The Grimshaws were concerned primarily with the manufacture of pure muriate of zinc and sizing ingredients, as well as chemicals required by India-rubber manufacturers. Part of the works had been taken over by Clayton Aniline by the mid-twentieth century.

Situated to the south-east of Clayton Aniline, and also occupying a canal-side site, was the Lindsey Chemical Works. This had become a rubber works by the 1950s. Other important works included Anderson's chemical works and the Anchor Chemical Works on Bank Street.

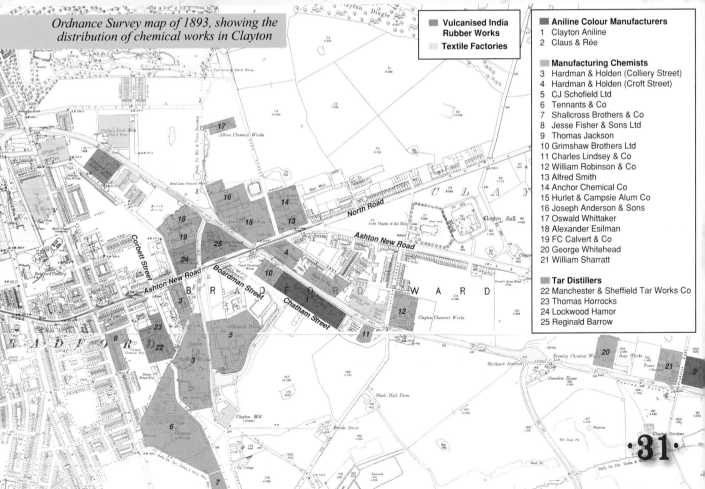

Ordnance Survey map of 1893, showing the distribution of chemical works in Clayton

Vulcanised India Rubber Works
Textile Factories

Aniline Colour Manufacturers
1 Clayton Aniline
2 Claus & Rée

Manufacturing Chemists
3 Hardman & Holden (Colliery Street)
4 Hardman & Holden (Croft Street)
5 CJ Schofield Ltd
6 Tennants & Co
7 Shallcross Brothers & Co
8 Jesse Fisher & Sons Ltd
9 Thomas Jackson
10 Grimshaw Brothers Ltd
11 Charles Lindsey & Co
12 William Robinson & Co
13 Alfred Smith
14 Anchor Chemical Co
15 Hurlet & Campsie Alum Co
16 Joseph Anderson & Sons
17 Oswald Whittaker
18 Alexander Esilman
19 FC Calvert & Co
20 George Whitehead
21 William Sharratt

Tar Distillers
22 Manchester & Sheffield Tar Works Co
23 Thomas Horrocks
24 Lockwood Hamor
25 Reginald Barrow

During the late eighteenth century, the ever-higher temperatures involved in industrial processes led to an increasing demand for refractory materials capable of withstanding and containing intense heat. Refractory bricks and crucibles were made from the fireclay that underlies most coal seams. Those that contained the highest proportion of alumina were considered to be the best, and it was for this reason that Stourbridge in the West Midlands and Halifax in Yorkshire emerged as early centres for manufacturing fire bricks.

The opportunity to manufacture refractory bricks from the fireclay that occurs in the Coal Measures at Clayton was seized by Robert Williams in *c* 1850, when he established a fire-brick works amidst the chemical works off Ashton New Road. Despite the growing demand for fire bricks from a wide range of industries locally, there were very few manufacturers of this specialised product in Manchester during the mid-nineteenth century. Robert Williams also manufactured a range of other products from the local fireclay, including chimney tops and 'sanitary wares', such as drain pipes.

Examples of fire bricks made by Williams & Co, and the Rake Fire Brick Co in Ancoats, that were discovered during the archaeological excavations

R. WILLIAMS & CO.,

MANUFACTURERS OF

FIRE BRICKS,

Chimney Tops, Sanitary Draining Pipes, &c.

ASHTON NEW ROAD, BRADFORD,

MANCHESTER.

Advertisement printed in Slater's trade directory for 1863

By the late 1870s, the fire-brick works had been taken over by Edward Williams, who was also manager of Bradford Colliery, and operated the Bradford Colliery brickworks. The fire-brick works is shown on historical mapping to have comprised two circular kilns and a long, narrow range, representing the drying shed. The fireclay, in the form of shale or rock, will have been gained from between the Openshaw and Charlotte coal seams via the 'shaft' that is marked in the southern part of the site. After a period of weathering in the yard, the initial processing would probably have taken place just to the north of the shaft, in the square-shaped building that is shown on historical mapping to have been open-sided.

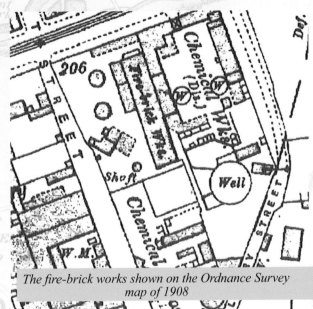

The fire-brick works shown on the Ordnance Survey map of 1908

The first stage in the production process was to crush the raw materials to a powder, for which an edge-runner mill was usually employed. The powder was then introduced to a pug mill, where it was mixed with liquid to form a plastic paste, ready to form into bricks. Fire-bricks were usually slop-moulded into shape, whereby a clot of clay was thrown by hand into a wet wooden mould. The brick was then taken to the drying shed, which was heated by either steam or under-floor flues.

A brick-moulder usually worked with assistants, who were responsible for preparing the clots of clay and carrying the bricks to the drying shed. Despite being a labour-intensive process, more than 3000 bricks could be prepared per day by this method. Once dried, the bricks could be transferred to the kiln, where they were fired at temperatures ranging from $1310^{\circ}C$ to $1800^{\circ}C$.

Late nineteenth-century edge-runner grinding mill, reproduced from a contemporary catalogue

The site of the fire-brick works was excavated in 2010-12. Whilst the southern part of the works was too contaminated with toxic industrial waste to allow a thorough examination, the top of the shaft was exposed. This was lined with bricks, and was approximately 3m in diameter. The foundations of two buildings that adjoined the open-sided processing shed just to the north of the shaft were also discovered. A substantial brick-built wall that crossed the centre of one of these buildings supported two huge stone blocks, which had clearly formed a solid foundation bed for a steam engine. This undoubtedly powered the winding gear that hoisted fireclay up the shaft. The engine will also have driven the edge-runner and pug mills in the open-sided building, which was probably an insubstantial structure, as excavation found no trace of any coherent foundations. An extensive brick surface was, however, revealed within the footprint of the building.

Excavating the floor of the open-sided processing shed

Excavation of the long, narrow range across the eastern part of the site revealed a floor of refractory tiles, each measuring 9in² and 2in deep (230 x 230 x 50mm). The tiles had been laid on a deposit of cinders, which overlay the natural geology. Immediately to the east of the floor were two parallel brick-lined channels, capped with specially moulded and interlocking refractory tiles. These channels were intended as flues, providing a conduit for hot gases through the building at floor level. This confirms that this part of the building had been a drying room, where freshly moulded 'green' bricks were dried gently prior to being fired in the kiln.

Refractory tile floor revealed in the drying shed along the eastern side of the works

Excavation revealed that only fragmentary remains of the kilns survived. These included a short, curved section of wall, which represented part of the outer wall of one of the kilns, and elements of the firing floor that was composed of two courses of hand-made bricks. Another short curved section of bricks in the centre of the kiln may have formed the vestiges of a flue, but severe ground contamination prevented further excavation of this area.

It seems from the evidence available that the kilns were of a circular, down-draught type, a design that was favoured by nineteenth-century fire-brick manufacturers as it was regulated more easily than other types. These kilns usually comprised up to ten evenly-spaced fire-mouths around the firing chamber, with a single doorway, or 'clammins', through which the brick-maker accessed the firing chamber.

The hot gases generated during firing were vented from the kiln via a well in the centre of the firing floor, which led to the chimney. These were often detached from the kilns, although some firms preferred to have an internal chimney as this produced a strong draught at the start of the firing process. It seems that Robert Williams & Co may have opted for this design, as the excavation produced no evidence for an external chimney, and nothing that can be identified as a chimney is shown on any historical mapping.

Williams' underground fireclay workings were abandoned in 1903, signalling the closure of the fire-brick works. This was replaced by a picture house, which was in use as a billiard hall by the 1920s, and finally as premises for Kay & Co, rainwear manufacturers.

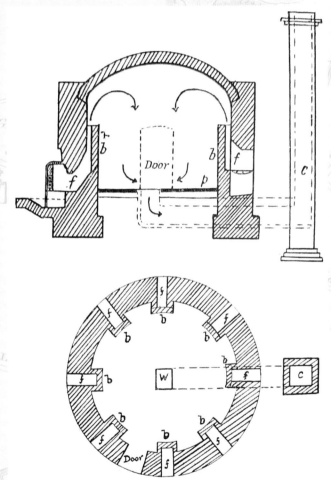

Plan and section of a down-draught kiln. The fireplaces (f) are set in the walls of the kiln, and heat rises through openings at the top of the bag-walls (b). The hot gases reflect against the dome-shaped roof and descend towards the centre of the floor (p), heating the bricks on contact. The gases are exhausted via the central well (w) to the chimney flue (c).

New industries were attracted to Clayton during the late nineteenth and early twentieth centuries, including the bicycle factory of the Manchester Cycle Manufacturing Company. Known originally as the Claviger Cycle Company Ltd, with a works on New Bridge Street in Manchester, the firm changed its name to the Manchester Cycle Manufacturing Company in December 1889. In 1890, the company increased its nominal capital from £21,000 to £50,000 to finance the construction

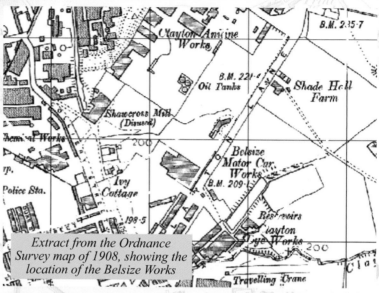

Extract from the Ordnance Survey map of 1908, showing the location of the Belsize Works

of the Belsize Works in Clayton, where it proceeded to develop a reputation for producing fine bicycles, which were exported throughout Britain.

Despite a boom in bicycle sales in 1895-6, the company went into receivership in 1897, with debts in excess of £12,200. The Belsize Works was purchased by Marshall & Co, and commenced business in the manufacture of motor vehicles. The first motor car to be produced at the Belsize Works was completed in 1897, and was the earliest car known to have been built in Manchester.

'The Irwell' safety bicycle, built in Clayton by the Manchester Cycle Manufacturing Company in the 1890s

The first model produced by Marshall & Co received a Gold Medal for efficiency at the 1899 London Exhibition. A new model, introduced in 1901, had a twin-cylinder engine, and was called the Marshall Belsize after the name of the firm's Clayton works. In 1903, the firm changed its name to Belsize Motor Cars & Engineering Co Ltd, and eventually to Belsize Motors Ltd.

A 1905 advertisement for Belsize motor cars

Up to the First World War, Belsize Motors Ltd was a leading manufacturer in the British motor-vehicle industry. The firm employed some 1200 people at their Belsize Works, and produced up to 50 vehicles a week, which included cars, taxis, fire engines and commercial vehicles fitted with engines of up to 14.5 litres capacity. The firm adopted American production techniques, pioneered by Henry Ford, although their vehicles remained hand-crafted and were therefore more expensive than some of their competitors.

The production line ceased temporarily in 1917-18, as the Belsize Works was given over to supplying munitions, adding to the significant contribution to the war effort afforded by Clayton's industrial base. The works reverted to manufacturing motor vehicles immediately after the war, although the company soon encountered financial difficulties, going into receivership in 1923, and finally ceased trading in 1925. The Belsize Works was taken over by Turner Automatic Machines Ltd, but by the early 1950s the buildings had been subsumed by an expansion of Clayton Aniline. Notwithstanding the historic importance of the site, it was not targeted for archaeological investigation, as it was considered most unlikely that any buried remains of significance would have survived the twentieth-century redevelopment.

The production floor at the Belsize Works in the early twentieth century

Munitions workers at the Belsize Works

HOUSING THE WORKFORCE

The population of Clayton had gradually risen to 1600 by 1859, but expanded steadily during the second half of the nineteenth century as local industries continued to develop. Much of the new housing for the influx of workers comprised rows of terraced properties, clustered along Ashton New Road, Edge Lane and Manchester Road, with slightly better-class houses along North Road. These added to the existing stock of more dispersed cottages, a sample of which was targeted for excavation.

Ivy Cottage

One of the earliest houses to be investigated was Ivy Cottage, which lay a short distance to the south of Clayton Mill. It is not known precisely when the cottage was built, although it is likely to have been intended to house agricultural workers prior to the onset of industrialisation. Artefacts recovered from the excavation date from the late eighteenth and nineteenth centuries, with no earlier material present. The pottery formed a domestic assemblage typical for this period, comprising a range of utilitarian vessels such as pancheons, storage jars, bottles, jugs, dishes, chamber pots and flower pots, together with some finer tablewares.

The cottage is depicted on the Ordnance Survey map of 1848 as a detached, square-shaped building fronting onto Colliery Lane. Additional documentary evidence for the first half of the nineteenth century is scant, although the Census returns for 1861 record two families living at Ivy Cottage: James Fildes, a farmer, together with his wife and son; and George Prestwidge, also a farmer, together with his wife and three daughters.

Excavation concluded that Ivy Cottage had been built as a small double-pile house. The typical plan form of a small rural cottage of this period comprised an offset doorway, providing access to two ground-floor rooms at the front of the property, with another two rooms to the rear. The layout of Ivy Cottage varied from this format slightly, with an offset entrance leading to a passageway that gave

The excavated foundations of Ivy Cottage

access to all the other rooms. The principal living room contained a large fireplace, set in the southern gable. On the opposite side of the passage was the parlour. Although generally associated with a function as a 'best' room, for entertaining, they originated as bedrooms, storerooms, dining rooms, and even workshops. The room would have had a fireplace, probably smaller than the functional hearth in the living room. The scullery was to the rear of the front rooms, with a back door that afforded access to the rear yard.

Remains of the fireplace in the living room

Newspaper articles printed in 1896-7 give Ivy Cottage as the residence of William Shawcross of Clayton Mill. Historical mapping shows that the building had been expanded to form an L-shaped plan by this date, with additional structure erected to the south-east, and a greenhouse in the rear garden. Excavation showed that the remodelling of the cottage included the addition of a service room and a new kitchen. The original flagstone flooring in the front two rooms was also replaced with a suspended timber floor, which became popular in the mid-nineteenth century. The fireplace in the living room was also modified, perhaps to allow a range to be installed.

The Census returns for 1911 list three families living at Ivy Cottage: Thomas Poyser, a farm labourer, together with his wife, daughter and niece; George Knowles, a farmer, together with his wife, brother and assistant, all of who were employed on a farm; and Oswald Stafford, a shoe repairer and pickle finisher, together with his wife. Ivy Cottage was eventually abandoned and demolished between 1922 and 1933, and the site was swallowed by an expansion of Clayton Aniline.

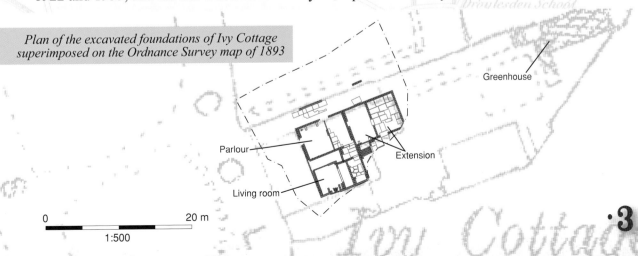

Plan of the excavated foundations of Ivy Cottage superimposed on the Ordnance Survey map of 1893

Greenhouse

Parlour

Extension

Living room

0   20 m

1:500

Cow Patch

Another block of cottages targeted for archaeological work was that named 'Cow Patch' on the Ordnance Survey map of 1848. These dwellings were built during the second quarter of the nineteenth century and, in contrast to Ivy Cottage, seem to have been intended to house a new industrial workforce. Census returns show that Cow Patch was occupied by ten individual households by 1871, and whilst the occupation of one resident is given as a farm labourer, most were employed in industry, and particularly coal mining. This connection is reinforced by the detail provided by Ordnance Survey mapping, which shows a track linking the cottages with Clayton Colliery and Clayton Mill.

Cow Patch cottages, shown on the Ordnance Survey map of 1848, with a track leading directly to Clayton Colliery and Clayton Mill

Evidence from the archaeological excavation demonstrated that Cow Patch had been erected as a block of single-roomed dwellings, built back-to-back. This plan form was very different from traditional rural workers' houses, such as Ivy Cottage, and whilst this type of building characterised the cheapest accommodation in mid-nineteenth-century Manchester, very few examples have been firmly identified in the surrounding rural fringe.

The remains of Cow Patch exposed during excavation

A flavour of the pre-industrial environment was provided from the scientific analysis of a buried soil that was sealed beneath the floor of the building range. Evidence from pollen spores pointed to a damp environment with some scrubby vegetation and areas of waste, open or cultivated ground. Amongst the plant species present were bristle club-rush, rushes, sedges, creeping buttercup, black bindweed, and nettles.

Despite the dramatic changes to the local environment brought about by industrial expansion in the nineteenth century, the Ordnance Survey map of 1893 shows that Cow Patch retained a rural aspect and was still surrounded by fields. The map depicts a row of four dwellings named 'Brooks Street', which excavation demonstrated to be a remodelled form of the original back-to-backs. The surviving foundations retained evidence for doorways having been inserted through partition walls, showing that the back-to-back cottages had been 'knocked through' to create a row of two-roomed dwellings. The Ordnance Survey map also shows a few detached outbuildings, including a row of four small structures just to the north of the cottages. Excavation confirmed that these were ash-pits or privies, with one for each house. These represent improvements in sanitation that were enacted progressively through legislation, both locally and nationally, during the second half of the nineteenth century.

Ordnance Survey mapping of 1908 shows the landscape was becoming more industrialised, with a major expansion of Clayton Aniline and the Belsize Motor Works. The persistence of Shade Hill Farm, situated a short distance to the north-east of Brooks Street, implies that agriculture still contributed to the local economy, however. Later mapping shows Shade Hill Farm to have been abandoned by 1922, and Brooks Street to have been subsumed by Clayton Aniline by the early 1950s.

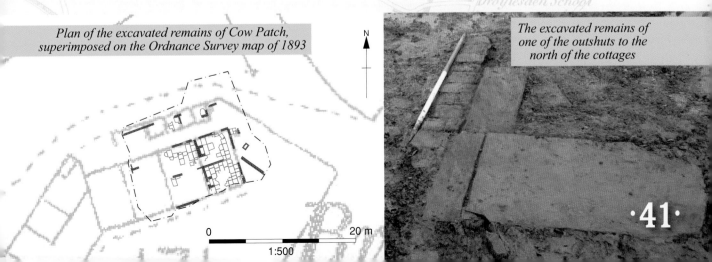

Plan of the excavated remains of Cow Patch, superimposed on the Ordnance Survey map of 1893

N

0   20 m

1:500

The excavated remains of one of the outshuts to the north of the cottages

Boardman Street

The remains of a different type of housing were excavated on Boardman Street, where a terrace of 14 dwellings was erected to the rear of properties on Ashton New Road in the 1850s. The 1861 Census shows that the residents of Boardman Street included labourers and managers, denoting a range of social levels residing in a similar standard of accommodation. The majority of the men and their sons worked in the local chemical or textile factories, with only one family of colliers.

Trial trenches placed across the site of workers' houses on Boardman Street

Initial trenches excavated across the footprint of the houses revealed well-preserved foundations buried beneath modern surfacing. Further excavation showed that all the houses were of a contemporary build, each comprising a main room with a narrow, single-storey outshut to the rear. This arrangement is somewhat uncommon for the mid-nineteenth century, although a similar plan type from the period *c* 1845-60 is known in Liverpool.

The front and rear walls of the excavated houses were of a full-brick thickness, although the partitions between the properties, and the outshuts to the rear, were only a half-brick wide. Each house will have had a window in the front wall, although physical evidence for the exact position did not survive, as the original wall had been reduced below windowsill level.

Excavating the full ground plan of workers' housing on Boardman Street

Fireplace

Doorway

The internal layout of each house was repeated, comprising a doorway at the south-eastern end of the front wall, and an off-centre fireplace on the north-western wall. Each main room was 13ft long and 11½ft wide (3.96 x 3.5m), with each outshut providing a 10ft long and 5ft wide space (3.05 x 1.52m) to the rear. It is likely that a steep, winding stair to the first floor had existed in the south-east corner of each main room, although all physical evidence had been removed.

The 1901 Census returns somewhat remarkably list 26 families residing on Boardman Street, with several also having lodgers to augment their income. This suggests that the houses had been sub-divided into single-roomed dwellings, with different families occupying the ground and first floors, and points to a decline in the prosperity of the locale, and a shortage of accommodation, with resultant overcrowding.

The houses had been demolished by 1908, although the front walls were retained as a boundary, with all the window and door apertures filled in. A new building was placed across the southern part of the plot, although this was also demolished within ten years to enable an embankment to be built for a railway line. This connected the chemical works on the south side of Ashton New Road with those to the north. Excavation showed that the ground level along Boardman Street was also raised at this time, burying the original flagstone pavement, and a new gas main was laid along the street. This cast-iron pipe retained the stamp of the Manchester Corporation Gas Works ('MCGW') and the date '1917'.

Fragment of a gas pipe laid in c 1917 as part of the redevelopment of Boardman Street

The archaeological excavations in Clayton were undertaken prior to the remediation works that were an essential stage in preparing the site of Clayton Aniline for a major redevelopment, which will enhance the existing suite of sporting facilities in the area, and contribute to the continued economic growth of East Manchester. The rejuvenation of this immense brownfield site provides another example in East Manchester of derelict and badly polluted land being regenerated successfully for future use.

One of the first major regeneration schemes of this type in the area was carried out by Manchester City Council in the early 1980s, and targeted Clayton Vale. Industry had abandoned this narrow stretch of the Irwell Valley by the 1920s, when it began to be used for large-scale tipping and landfill purposes. This continued into the 1970s, and resulted in the polluted degradation of Clayton Vale's landscape. The large scheme of remediation and restoration of the area took several years to complete, but has ultimately provided a pleasant landscape setting and wildlife haven, with a network of paths for walkers and the planting of approximately 250,000 native trees and bushes.

View across the ravaged Clayton Vale in 1963

Modern view across the regenerated Clayton Vale

In 1999, the New East Manchester Partnership was established and formulated a long-term strategy to reverse the economic and social decline of East Manchester. A significant catalyst to the ensuing regeneration of the area was provided by the Commonwealth Games, held in Manchester in 2002, which brought a suite of new sporting venues to the area, including the City of Manchester Stadium, the Manchester Velodrome and the National Squash Centre.

More recently, in 2010, Manchester City Football Club (MCFC) entered an agreement with the City Council and New East Manchester to allow a £1 billion redevelopment of derelict land around their stadium. This commenced with the remediation and site-servicing works required to prepare the sites of the former Bradford Colliery and Bradford Ironworks for new uses, coupled with an archaeological excavation of the historic industrial remains (see *Greater Manchester's Past Revealed*, **4**).

Following the completion of this major scheme of works, MCFC progressed the remediation of contaminated land that had been occupied by Clayton Aniline and the OMG Works, in advance of the club's regeneration of the site for additional sporting facilities. As with the earlier scheme, the groundwork was preceded by a programme of archaeological investigation that aimed to record any buried remains of the area's rich industrial heritage prior to their ultimate loss.

Whilst contaminated ground is frequently an issue to be considered when proposing the excavation of former industrial complexes, the site of Clayton Aniline and the OMG Works presented significant challenges. The site was subject to a detailed quantitative risk assessment as an initial stage of the scheme, which identified the location and extent of ground contaminants of concern. The long list of chemicals that was recognised included benzene, nitrobenzene, toluene, phenol, and naphthalene, all deriving from the former industrial use of the site. Archaeological excavation was not carried out in the localised areas where significant concentrations of these chemicals were identified, and necessary precautions were taken in all other areas, although in some cases the appropriate course of action was to cease excavation.

The archaeological work at Clayton Aniline was carried out by OA North to satisfy planning conditions for the development. Manchester City Council attached these conditions to planning consent on the recommendation of the Greater Manchester Archaeological Advisory Service, which also devised a specification for the scope of works required, and provided advice through the entire process from starting the initial evaluation trenching through to final publication. The archaeological work was intended to make a detailed and accurate record of any important buried remains that had survived within the site. This process is known as 'preservation by record' and it leads to the creation of a technical report and site archive. This approach is in accordance with current national planning policies on the conservation of the historic environment, which are set out in the National Planning Policy Framework (NPPF). The NPPF also stresses the importance of making the information generated from archaeological investigations publicly available. The intention of this booklet has been to achieve this aspiration.

GLOSSARY

ANILINE: a colourless, oily, poisonous benzene derivative used in the manufacture of dyes, resins, pharmaceuticals, varnishes and rubber.

CHAPMAN a derivative of the Saxon word 'Caepman', meaning a marketman, monger, or merchant.

COAL TAR: a brown or black liquid of extremely high viscosity derived as a by-product from the carbonisation of coal. In chemical terms, coal tars are complex and variable mixtures of phenols, polycyclic aromatic hydrocarbons, and heterocyclic compounds.

CRUCK: a cruck or crook frame is a curved timber, one of a pair, which supports the roof of a building. This type of timber framing consists of long, bent, timber beams that lean inwards and form the ridge of the roof.

FIRE BRICK: a block of refractory ceramic material used in lining furnaces, kilns and fireplaces.

FUSTIAN: a strong, twilled cloth, with a linen warp and a cotton weft.

GALLIGU: the waste material from the Leblanc process of manufacturing soda, comprising a mixture of mainly calcium sulphide, with lesser amounts of unburnt coal, coal ash and sodium sulphide.

MINE INSPECTORS: the Coal Mines Inspection Act of 1850 aimed to address the frequency of accidents in mines, and introduced the appointment of inspectors of coal mines, placing them under the supervision of the Home Office.

PIT BANK: the raised ground or platforms upon which the coals are sorted and screened at the surface.

SLOP MOULDING: a method of forming bricks using moulds that have been soaked in water to prevent the clay from sticking to the sides.

FURTHER READING

Abrahart, E N, 1976 *The Clayton Aniline Company Ltd, 1876-1976*, Preston

Campbell, W A, 1971 *The Chemical Industry*, London

Cronin, J, and Rhodes, F, 2005 *Clayton and Openshaw*, Stroud

Higson, J, 1859 *Historical and Descriptive Notices of Droylsden, Past and Present*, Manchester

Miller, I, 2011 *Rediscovering Bradford: Archaeology in the Engine Room of Bradford, Greater Manchester's Past Revealed*, **4**, Lancaster

Walker, J S F, and Tindall, A S (eds), 1985 *Country Houses of Greater Manchester, The Archaeology of Greater Manchester*, **2**, Manchester

All of the historical maps used in this booklet can be found at Manchester Archives and Local Studies, Manchester Central Library. Historical images can also be view on at http://images.manchester.gov.uk

A copy of each of the detailed excavation reports has been deposited with the Greater Manchester Historic Environment Record.

Other books in the *Greater Manchester's Past Revealed* series:

Piccadilly Place: Uncovering Manchester's Industrial Origins – **1**

The Rock Triangle, Bury: The Archaeology of an Industrial Suburb – **2**

Discovering Coccium: The Archaeology of Roman Wigan – **3**

Rediscovering Bradford: Archaeology in the Engine Room of Manchester – **4**

Slices Through Time: Greater Manchester's Historic Character Revealed – **5**

An Industrial Art: The Archaeology of Calico Printing in the Irwell Valley – **6**

Newton Hall: Rediscovering a Manorial Complex – **7**

Timperley Old Hall: Greater Manchester's Historic Character Revealed – **8**